QUANTUM LEARNER

Focus Your Energy, Get What You Want

Bobbi DePorter

Welcome to the
Quantum Upgrade Book Series

Do you have times when you can't seem to make things
turn out the way you want at school or in your life?
No matter how hard you study, you can't do better on
a test? You want to earn more respect from a friend,
parent or teacher but you don't know how? You want
to be more independent or change how someone feels
about you, but what you're doing isn't working? Now
think of the opposite times when things just click.
Everything just falls into place – and before you know
it you're flowing ahead to the next thing. You seem to
catch success after success. The truth is, you're a
natural learner, made for these moments.

In today's quantum world you need fast skills and vast
knowledge to learn more, be more and do more. Use
your quantum upgrade to be in control of how you feel,
think and learn, and take more personal responsibility
for running your life.

The Quantum Upgrade Book Series:

Quantum Learner
Quantum Reader
Quantum Writer
Quantum Memorizer
Quantum Thinker
Quantum Note-Taker

QUANTUM LEARNER

Focus Your Energy, Get What You Want

LEARNING FORUM PUBLICATIONS

Published by Learning Forum Publications

Submit all requests for reprinting to:

Learning Forum Publications
1938 Avenida del Oro
Oceanside, CA 92056
(760) 722-0072

Cover and interior design: Stephen Schildbach
Illustrations: Jonathan Fischer
Book concept: John Pederson
Editor: Sue Baechler

Library of Congress Control Number: 2006940414

ISBN-10: 0-945525-41-9
ISBN-13: 978-0-945525-41-7

Printed in the United States of America

To the Quantum Learner who wants to learn more,
be more and do more in school and life.

Enjoy all six of our books:
Quantum Learner, Quantum Reader,
Quantum Writer, Quantum Memorizer,
Quantum Thinker and Quantum Note-Taker.

Contents

Becoming a Quantum Learner

You were born with a quantum brain. You were also born a learner. Your brain is a storehouse of natural learning energy and experiences. Learning is everything you do with it. You are always learning how to feel, how to change how you feel, how to think about something, how to do something new or differently, and how to understand more. Big and little changes are happening in your brain every moment, sculpting how you experience your life.

1

> **Quantum learners picture themselves successful.**

As a quantum learner, you can turn every opportunity to learn and perform into a successful experience just by the way you think about it, get ready for it, and take responsibility. Whether you're taking a test or trying something new, improving a paper or a talent, making a presentation or a new friend – you can learn to control outcomes to make more things go your way.

In chapter one you'll find out how to expect and get more positive results in school and life. And with more successes, you're willing to try new things and set bigger goals. Chapter two helps you figure out all the ways you're already smart and how your brain learns best. In chapter three, you'll upgrade learning skills for remembering anything, expressing your thoughts, studying smarter, test-taking, writing more easily, and reading faster. You'll learn how to focus your new skills and learning energy in chapter four with eight keys for living a responsible life.

What if you could be the
sculptor of your life experiences
and control where your learning
energy goes to get more of the things
you want? That's what being a
quantum learner is all about.

Chapter 1:

Expect Your Best Results

☐ Your upgrade is in progress

Think of the most difficult subjects you've ever had in school. Imagine all the books, handouts and notes for what you were studying stacked in front of you. Now imagine a stack of books and papers 100 times larger than that – large enough to fill an entire room. That's how much you learned just to take your first step as a child. Learning to talk was even more complex. Despite the size of these tasks, there was never any question of whether you'd be able to do it. You, and everyone around you, expected success – and that's exactly what happened.

Fast forward to today.

What kind of results do you expect at school and in life? If you had a pile of books in front of you right now, would you expect to learn them in a day? A week? A month?

When you're learning something new, do you think about the *ifs* or do you focus your energy on the *when* and *how*?

> To get what you want in life, focus your energy on when and how, not if.

Focusing on the *when* and *how* is the faster and more natural way to expect and get your best results. It shifts how you feel, think and learn into *I can*, *I want to*, and *I will* success mode. You picture yourself successful – which is just what you did as a child when you picked your moment, stood up and toddled across the room that first time.

Expecting your best and picturing success also means you have to move out of your comfort zone and anticipate challenges and take risks. That's what the learning zone is all about.

Get Into Learning
• Get grades that get noticed.
• Get friends that 'get you'.
• Get focused on what you want.

Go For It!

Getting the best results often means taking a risk to try something new. When you do, you're not totally sure how things will turn out, but you go for it anyway. You have to create your own momentum to get from the *wanting* to the *getting*. The stuff in the middle is where learning takes place – it's called the Learning Zone. It's where you make a jump from *wanting* to *getting* – from your comfort zone to better grades, friends and life experiences.

Think of it this way:

Remember the first time you tried to do something new like rollerblading, skateboarding, playing an instrument, or mastering a new software application? Whatever it was, you expected that you could get the

results you wanted if you stuck with it, and that's what happened. Eventually, you went for it and got what you focused on! But you had to push yourself through a period of risks and challenges to get there – that's the learning zone.

Quantum learners love to learn.

Let's say you were learning to rollerblade. At first, you probably didn't feel very cool or confident. But you stepped out of your comfort zone by putting on your blades and awkwardly making your way down the sidewalk. You fell a few times, picked yourself up, adjusted your technique, and off you went. You were in the zone – the learning zone. When you're in the learning zone, you're stretching into a new space that gives you the confidence to try new things.

Try this:

Draw a square and write the words comfort zone inside. Then think of the kinds of things you do at school and in life that are inside that zone. Now, draw four arrows out from each corner of the square into a big unknown space – your learning zone. Think of the things you would do if you were confident that you could achieve them. Would you join new groups at school, make a new friend, try out for a school play or sports team, run for class officer, learn another language?

What's in your learning zone?

Learn Your ABCs

Whether you're rollerblading, writing a book report, or improving a relationship with a friend, you can get more of what you want by shifting your ABCs: Attitude, Belief and Concentration. Think of these as your ABCs of learning at a whole new level.

Attitude Has Everything to Do With Energy and Results

You always hear people talking about attitude: I like your attitude! That's not the right attitude, etc. But what is attitude, really?

Your attitude is closely related to your opinions. It's about you and your thoughts about things, not something outside of you. It's the powerful combination of your emotions and actions. For quantum learners, it's a contagious can-do feeling that seeps into everything you see, say, think and touch. Your attitude is a force field that gives you confidence and positively influences how other people feel being around you.

A positive attitude helps you focus your emotions and actions on getting what you want. A negative attitude means that your emotions and actions are taking you in the opposite direction – it's that simple.

Shifting your attitude into positive mode doesn't mean that you had a bad attitude to start with; it just means that you have the power to get better results.

Here's how to make the shift:

Your brain listens to your body. Do you know that your thinking and feeling are connected to your body's actions? You act how you feel, and you feel how you act makes sense, right? And unlike feelings and thinking, physical actions are easier to change. When you adjust your body, it's surprising how your thoughts and feelings fall in line to support the shift. I like to say: *Change one, change all three.* When your mind, body and emotions all come together, you suddenly see new solutions as well as the problems. You see new paths forward.

Have you ever tried to get a group or team psyched for a game or project? That's your attitude in action: You're turning your positive thoughts and emotions into words and actions that build expectations for the best results. If the game or project is important to you, you let it show by organizing a practice or study group. You show everyone that you're expecting the best. It's more likely that they will respond positively too – and more likely you'll have a good team result. You know this works the opposite way too. If you start out thinking that your team will never get into the project as much as you will and you'll end up doing all the work – that's probably what will happen because your negative attitude has set lower expectations.

The secret is that your brain listens to your body – whether you want it to or not. If you're slouching in your chair, your body sends your brain an instant message that says: "This is boring. You don't need to know this." Your brain sends one back that says, "OK, C U L8R!" and goes offline to daydream.

But you can use the same high-speed connection to line up your feelings and actions with a positive attitude.

Simply changing the way you sit in a chair, walk down a hallway, or enter a room, can shift your feelings and help you realize new possibilities.

Try this:

Walk tall into your classroom. Notice how you feel different instantly. Just this action changes a lot.

You can get your brain and your body into a positive attitude for learning any time. Do these three things to trigger changes in your body chemistry that will help you take control of how you feel, think and act:

1. **Adjust your physiology.** (Sit tall, walk tall.)
2. **Breathe from your belly.** (Take slow, deep breaths that calm you.)
3. **Look and listen.** (Pay attention.)

A positive attitude is like a battery charger for your best results, but you also need energy straight from the source: belief in yourself and what you want.

You Better Believe It!

Do you believe that there are 50 states in the U.S.? Do you believe that there are other in- habited planets like Earth? That Jimmi Hendrix was the best guitar player ever? Do you believe that you'll be able to dunk a basketball someday?

When you believe in something, it automatically shifts your thinking and makes it real in your mind. It changes your reality. Suddenly, you spend more time practicing because you can picture yourself on a slam-dunk breakaway. Belief is what makes your expectations real. It's what helps you see the best results in your mind, giving you a vision of success so you can raise the bar on your results.

You may already know about the SLANT method for quickly adjusting your attitude and getting your best results. We adapted it from Dr. Ed Ellis, and it's always worth a reminder.

SLANT stands for Sit up in your chair, Lean forward, Ask questions, Nod your head, and Talk to your teacher. It's a simple and powerful way to take advantage of your body and brain connection and focus more of your learning power.

Simply changing the way you sit and listen to information will totally shift how your brain takes in the information. When you use SLANT, your body triggers your brain to get online and focus on what's happening. It's like calling your friend up to say, "You gotta see this!"

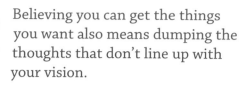

Believing you can get the things you want also means dumping the thoughts that don't line up with your vision.

When you have positive attitudes and beliefs about yourself and learning, you feel closer to the things you want. Concentration is the laser focus that helps you get what you want.

The Big "C": Concentration

According to the dictionary, concentration means focusing all your thoughts and energy on one task. According to quantum learners, concentration means focusing all your thoughts and energy to get the results you want. Staring at a book or lesson until your eyes bug out may be good enough for the dictionary, but it's not good enough for quantum learners – so it's not good enough for you!

As a quantum learner, you'll use a specific type of concentration, called alpha state, to focus your learning energy.

> Quantum learners are motivated and confident.

Fimage is Fear of Image. It's something you want to get rid of in your life. Fear of image happens when the person you dress up and act like every day is not totally true to the person you are inside. A lot of people end up acting out an image because they fear they won't be liked and appreciated for who they really are. When you get rid of that fimage (fear of image) it's like lifting a big weight off your body. You free yourself to be your true self. It's not easy to lose fimage, but it's a step toward getting what you want in life that all quantum learners take.

Learners love alpha state

We all know what concentration feels like: a tractor beam of focused energy pulling you toward your goal. But do you know what it looks like? Look at the line on the next page that represents alpha waves. Scientists actually measure and map out different wavelengths and have identified the alpha state as the most effective for learning.

17

Here's a rundown of the four main categories, or states, of brainwave activity:

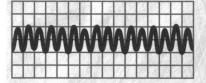

Beta—Awake, alert, and active. In beta, your brain is attending to many different stimuli at once. Activity is scattered. You may be thinking of many things at the same time or jumping from one activity to another. Four Instant Message conversations at once – that's your beta waves at work.

Alpha—A state of relaxed concentration. You're calm and alert, absorbing material and making connections. You are 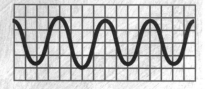 completely focused on one activity. It could be your favorite sitcom or a challenging game of chess. This is the best state for learning. Quantum readers ride alpha waves wherever they want to go.

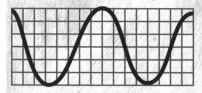

Theta—Your brainwaves are slowing down, just seconds away from a deep sleep. This is where you dream and process information.

Delta—The slowest brainwave state. You're in a deep sleep.

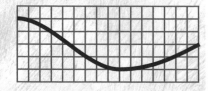

18

Think of it this way:

There's one state where the best learning happens, called the alpha state. Every time you want to learn something, you'll want to take a little road trip to get there.

Directions to Alpha State:	Distance to Destination:

1: Get into alpha state by sitting up, taking a deep breath, closing your eyes and letting them roll up.

.87 Quantum miles

2: Picture yourself in a favorite place where you feel relaxed and peaceful. This could be a special room in your home, your favorite park, a beach – anywhere that you're totally comfortable and know well enough to picture yourself there in your mind. What does it look, smell and feel like? See yourself there now.

.53 Quantum miles

3: Open your eyes to find yourself in the alert and calm state of alpha brainwaves. Now you can completely focus on your material or event.

You have arrived!

Theta brainwaves lock in learning

Wish you could study while you sleep? Well, in a way you can! Quantum learners want all the advantages they can get from the way their brain naturally works. Brain researchers have learned that we process our thoughts and learnings during the night and that our brains focus on the thoughts we had closest to falling asleep. Their experience with students tells us that if students study, then watch TV, play video games, etc., these activities interfere with the brain's ability to lock in what they studied.

If, instead, students take a quick scan of their school-work before falling asleep, it can make a big difference in what they remember and their understanding of what they studied. Teachers even say that test scores go up when students scan their studies just before they go to sleep.

We call this the Theta Scan because it's happening during your theta brainwave activity time – a reminder to scan your studies last to get the full benefit of all the time you put in already. Try out the Theta Scan to get extra hours of your brain focusing on your studies.

As a quantum learner, you know about your learning zone and how to take on challenges, and you are aware of the power of your attitude, beliefs and self-image. You also know how to focus your concentration, but it takes commitment to get the value out of all of your learning energy.

Make a Committment

A commitment is like a promise to yourself that you put a lot of energy into. Quantum learners make a commitment to give their best effort to get their best results.

If this is what you want for yourself, write it down and put it where you will see it every day – "I give my best effort to get my best results."

When you make a commitment to give your best effort and expect your best results, you realize how much more control you have in getting what you want in school and life. And now you have techniques for shifting into a positive attitude, believing in your best results, and getting into a state for better concentration and more effective learning.

Use the next chapter to choose the best paths forward for getting what you want. You'll discover your personal learning style and make a big list of how you're already smart.

Chapter 2:

Know How You Learn Best – Learn Better!

Your upgrade is 25% complete

Knowing how you learn best offers pathways to effective learning and living. Here are three ways you can discover how you learn best:

1. Determine your personal learning style (modality)
2. Be aware of your focus – external or internal?
3. Know how you're already smart (multiple intelligences)

Get Smart, Get the Facts

Fact: Every person is smart.
Fact: People learn differently.
Fact: When you find out how you learn,
you feel smart.

Determining your personal learning style means knowing how everything you experience enters your brain and naturally makes sense to you. When you know that your learning-style preference is visual (seeing), auditory (hearing), or kinesthetic (moving/touching), you set yourself up for more success. Being aware of your focus gives you valuable insight into your own reactions and those of others and will help you learn better when combined with your knowledge of your learning style and how you're already smart. Knowing how you're already smart (like people smart, word smart, picture smart, etc.) is an exciting adventure into the multiple intelligences that make you special.

Whether you play a sport or an instrument, or you like to make things or write stories, you try to maximize your effort and ability by choosing strategies that emphasize your strengths. The same is true with learning. If you want better results, you have to play to your strengths. The VAK (visual, auditory, kinesthetic) model is one way to do that.

It's true that no single learning style description can totally describe you as an individual. But if you know your brain's preference for learning, you can use this knowledge to arrange information to fit your brain. This means you'll "get" new information faster by putting it into the style that your brain likes. It's like choosing a pair of running shoes: You can get to the finish line faster by choosing a size and style that work best for you!

How do you prefer to take in info? Check out your learning style.

What Kind of Learner Are You?

Imagine you just bought a new drum set or tent that comes in twenty different pieces, accompanied by a twelve-page instruction booklet to help you assemble it. What's your next move? Does everything you read in the booklet seem vague and unclear until you look at the illustration and start putting the pieces together yourself? Or does the opposite happen: You're baffled by the array of parts, but when you read the instructions, everything seems perfectly clear.

If you need to start working with the parts physically, you're probably a kinesthetic learner: You learn by touch, feel and movement. If reading the instructions or looking at the drawings clarifies things for you, you're most likely visual. If you can't make it work from pictures, but when you call the company and someone tells you how to put the thing together, it all begins to make sense – that's a definite clue that your style is auditory.

Let's have a closer look at these learning styles:

Visual

Do you doodle when you talk on the phone? Do you need to see info, either in writing or in charts, graphs or pictures to remember it? Would you rather see a map than hear directions? Do you use expressions like:

- *Picture this*
- *I see what you mean*
- *Focus here*

If you answered yes to these questions, you're probably a visual learner.

Auditory

Do you talk to yourself? I mean, do you repeat information out loud to remember it? Can you follow lectures easily just by hearing the words? Would you rather listen to the radio than read the newspaper? Do you learn languages easily by hearing native speakers? Do you use expressions like:

- *Sounds like*
- *Rings a bell*
- *Listen*
- *I hear you loud and clear*

If you answered yes to these questions, you're probably an auditory learner.

Kinesthetic

Are you a hands-on learner? Do you think better when you're moving and walking around? Do you need to demonstrate ideas with movements and act them out? Do you say things like:

- *Grasp the concept*
- *Get a handle on it*
- *I'm touched*
- *Slipped my mind*

If you answered yes to these questions, you're probably a kinesthetic learner.

You have just learned one important part of your learning style – your modality or how your brain prefers to take in information. Have fun taking the Modality Survey on the next page to find out the details about how you learn best.

(You can find out even more about your learning style by discovering how your brain likes to organize and process information in another book in this series, Quantum Thinker.*)*

When I was in school I had trouble learning languages. They were so easy for other people, but not me. I took Spanish in high school. I'd hear it spoken and try to repeat it, but I just couldn't get it to stick. I thought there must be something wrong with my brain. But when I tried writing out the words and making myself a set of flash cards to go with the lesson, I started getting somewhere. The activities of forming the words with my hands and writing the words down made the information visual so it stuck in my head. I realized that I was a low auditory learner and I had a smart visual and kinesthetic brain. Have you had experiences like this where you thought you couldn't learn something and then you tried another way and you got it? That's the value of VAK – knowing how your brain prefers to take in information and making your life and learning easier by giving your brain what it wants!

Modality Survey

Directions: Select A, B or C based on the word group or sentence you like the best. Circle the letter of your selection. Then transfer your selections to the Modality Data Sheet on the next page and follow instructions to get your Modality Profile.

1. **A.** Rustling–Hear–Tempo | **B.** Texture–Feel–Soft | **C.** Illustration–Picture–Snapshot
2. **A.** I get it | **B.** I see | **C.** I hear you
3. **A.** I heard the train whistle | **B.** I saw the rows of flowers | **C.** I felt the breeze on my back
4. **A.** Focus–Color–Impact | **B.** Chat–Stillness–Tune | **C.** Race–Latch–Loosen
5. **A.** Bird's-eye view | **B.** Rings true | **C.** Hang in there
6. **A.** Nod–Glide–Signal | **B.** Shiny–Reflection–Attractive | **C.** Call–Whisper–Bell
7. **A.** This sounds good to me | **B.** This feels good to me | **C.** This looks good to me
8. **A.** Vision–Clear–Glimpse | **B.** Melody–Quiet–Hear | **C.** Touch–Smooth–Movement
9. **A.** I sense how you feel | **B.** I hear what you're saying | **C.** I see what you mean
10. **A.** Peek–Sight–View | **B.** Scoot–Gallop–Skip | **C.** Describe–Song–Chime
11. **A.** Get in touch with | **B.** Appears to me | **C.** Loud and clear
12. **A.** Lend me an ear | **B.** Keep an eye out | **C.** Give him a hand
13. **A.** The sport was fun | **B.** The sunset was beautiful | **C.** It was music to my ears
14. **A.** Grip–Support–Relax | **B.** Mention–Tone–Rhyme | **C.** Show–Notice–Dream
15. **A.** It sounded good | **B.** It felt good | **C.** It looked good
16. **A.** Look at this | **B.** Catch this | **C.** Listen up
17. **A.** Purring–Listen–Talk | **B.** Glow–Appear–See | **C.** Hold–Trot–Catch
18. **A.** Clear as a bell | **B.** Smooth as silk | **C.** Bright as day
19. **A.** The feel of the sand | **B.** The view of the ocean | **C.** The sound of the waves
20. **A.** Look–Color–Glance | **B.** Upbeat–Speak–Sound | **C.** Motion–Lukewarm–Sprint
21. **A.** Let me hear this | **B.** Let me do this | **C.** Let me see this
22. **A.** The sight on the stage | **B.** The sound of the instruments | **C.** The vibration in the air
23. **A.** Discuss–Silence–Say | **B.** Watch–Shine–Observe | **C.** Run–Throw–Snap
24. **A.** The sound had an interesting melody | **B.** The cloth had a smooth feel | **C.** The painting had beautiful colors
25. **A.** A glimpse of... | **B.** Hear the sound of... | **C.** In touch with...

Modality Data Sheet

Directions: Transfer your responses from the Modality Survey to this data sheet by placing a circle around the letter. Count the number of letters circled and enter the total at the bottom of each column.

1.	C	A	B
2.	B	C	A
3.	B	A	C
4.	A	B	C
5.	A	B	C
6.	B	C	A
7.	C	A	B
8.	A	B	C
9.	C	B	A
10.	A	C	B
11.	B	C	A
12.	B	A	C
13.	B	C	A
14.	C	B	A
15.	C	A	B
16.	A	C	B
17.	B	A	C
18.	C	A	B
19.	B	C	A
20.	A	B	C
21.	C	A	B
22.	A	B	C
23.	B	A	C
24.	C	A	B
25.	A	B	C

TOTAL 1	TOTAL 2	TOTAL 3
X4=		

Put the total from each column in the first row of boxes, multiply each total by 4 and enter that amount in the second row of boxes. Then graph your results on the Modality Profile on the next page. (Developed by John Parks Le Tellier, educational consultant and Quantum Learning instructor)

33

Modality Profile

1.	Visual										
		10	20	30	40	50	60	70	80	90	

2.	Auditory										
		10	20	30	40	50	60	70	80	90	

3.	Kinesthetic										
		10	20	30	40	50	60	70	80	90	

Do You Focus More on Other People or on Your Own Thoughts?

Now that you know how your brain takes in information, let's figure out whether you're internally or externally focused. Awareness of your personal focus can help you understand your reactions and be comfortable with how you react in different situations. It can also enhance your learning by helping you to seek learning situations that fit your focus preference – such as finding a quiet place to study by yourself or arranging to meet with groups for a more lively exchange of information.

Now let's look at your focus:

Imagine that you've just been cast into your favorite reality show. To survive, you need to work with members of your team to achieve different objectives or missions. It's really not all that different from real life. I guess that's why they call it reality television!

You'll notice that some people in the group naturally leap to action without much hesitation. They're totally focused on what everyone else is doing – on what is happening within the group. These people have external focus. Other members of the group sit back and carefully consider their next move before taking action. They're more concerned with their contribution than with what's going on with the group as a whole. These people are internally focused. Which is more like you?

Knowing the difference between internal and external focus helps you concentrate your learning energy because you can anticipate how you will react to different situations. It also helps you see things the way other people may be looking at them and respect the intention behind their actions. Bottom line: Knowing the difference between internal and external focus will help you learn better on your own and with other people. This is another powerful way to know yourself.

Know How You're Already Smart

We are all smart in different ways – eight different ways according to multiple intelligence expert, Howard Gardner.

Knowing how you're already smart, and making a list to remind yourself, is one of the biggest positive boosts to your learning energy. Taking this inventory of your intelligences is a fun side-trip into who you are as a learner and what makes you strong as a person.

Take the Smart Chart Survey to make your own big Smart Chart and see the intelligences you already have.

What's On Your Smart Chart?

 Spatial
(Picture Smart)

 Naturalistic
(Nature Smart)

 Linguistic
(Word Smart)

 Bodily
(Body Smart)

 Interpersonal
(People Smart)

 Intrapersonal
(Self Smart)

 Musical
(Music Smart)

 Mathematical
(Number Smart)

Smart Chart Survey

DIRECTIONS: Circle the actions you like to do, or do well.

 1. Competing in a sport

 2. Listening to others' opinions and feelings

 3. Collecting things and organizing them

 4. Daydreaming or visualizing

 5. Acting, role playing and mimicking

 6. Playing musical instruments

 7. Doing problem-solving quizzes in magazines

 8. Learning about other cultures

 9. Looking for patterns in the stars

 10. Spending time alone thinking things through

 11. Telling jokes and stories

 12. Imagining things in my head in pictures

 13. Singing almost anywhere

 14. Figuring out the reasons for things

 15. Browsing through books

 16. Fixing, assembling and building

 17. Putting puzzles together

37

18. Doing my part when I'm part of a team project

 19. Dealing with my own feelings

 20. Doing math in my head

 21. Arranging CDs in a specific order

 22. Listening to music

 23. Doing experiments

 24. Reading

 25. Resolving conflicts or arguments

 26. Sharing with others

 27. Using music to change my mood or feelings

 28. Exercising

 29. Painting, drawing or sketching

 30. Learning plant names and families

 31. Finding my way using a map

 32. Dancing or playing games that require movement

 33. Working out the answers to logical arguments

 34. Giving encouragement and positive support to others

35. Writing

36. Doing spot-the-difference puzzles

37. Knowing my sources of strength

38. Making up songs

39. Telling others about what I have read

40. Doodling in my notes

Your Smart Chart

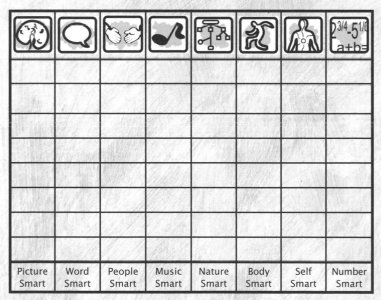

Picture Smart	Word Smart	People Smart	Music Smart	Nature Smart	Body Smart	Self Smart	Number Smart

DIRECTIONS: For every item you circled, look at the symbol associated with that item and color in one box (starting at the bottom of the column).

Example: If you circled three musical symbols, you'd color in three places in the Music Smart column. The columns with the most boxes colored in represent all the ways you are already smart.

How does your Smart Chart help you learn? Here are some examples:

If you're **Picture Smart**, you use drawing and doodling to learn faster and better. Your active imagination is great for reading, writing, thinking and memorizing, and you understand how things connect, go together, and fit with each other.

If you're **Word Smart**, you use stories to learn. You're great at writing and making up poems and rhymes, and easily learn other languages.

If you're **People Smart**, you are friendly and learn by communicating with other people. You know how to make friends feel better, and you can organize a team to make anything happen.

If you're **Music Smart**, you've got rhythm and you find lots of ways to make music, like humming and whistling. You can learn to play instruments easily and you pick up and remember songs and sounds all the time.

If you're **Nature Smart,** you learn very actively by finding out how things work and what's different about them. Puzzles and patterns are easy for you to spot and you like to categorize items in groups to make sense of them.

If you're **Body Smart**, you like to experience learning through movement. You're naturally good at dancing

and sports and you've got very coordinated hands and fingers for making things.

If you're **Self Smart**, you are a confident learner because you know what you're good at and how to get what you want. You are disciplined and focused and your self-understanding makes you a strong personality who takes control.

If you're **Number Smart**, you're skillful at solving problems and working with numbers. You are a naturally curious learner and like to question why things happen and how things work.

41

Knowing how you're already smart also helps you upgrade your learning skills (like reading, writing, memorizing and test-taking) because you are more aware of what comes naturally to you (like music, words, pictures, athletics, numbers) and how to make learning new things more fun.

By combining and applying your knowledge of your personal learning style, your focus, and how you're already smart, you will know how you learn best, learn better – and get what you go after.

Knowing how you
learn best offers pathways
to effective learning
and living.

What kind of learner are you?

Chapter 3:
Upgrade Your Learning Skills

Your upgrade is 50% complete

Knowing how you learn and how you're smart will get you your best results and more of the things you want in school and life. Upgrading your learning skills will help you learn faster and gain the knowledge you need to pursue what interests and excites you for your whole life.

In this chapter you'll learn key techniques, tools and strategies for faster and more focused studying and learning.

Learning skills are core activities like reading, writing, studying, test-taking, note-taking, thinking and memorizing. You can find out even more about each of these core activities in the other Quantum Upgrade books: *Quantum Reader*, *Quantum Writer*, *Quantum Memorizer*, *Quantum Thinker* and *Quantum Note-Taker*.

The tools you use to upgrade your learning are like the tools you'd find in your garage or workshop – at least you can think of them that way. Some are simple and their benefits are instantly available, like that of a screwdriver. Others, like a jigsaw, take a little more practice before you can use them well. This chapter focuses mostly on the screwdriver skills that you can use to upgrade your learning right now.

Get ready for better results with faster skills that use your brain more efficiently.

Get Better Skills

Know how to learn fast.
Know how to do well on tests.
Know how to study without stress.

Three Big Brain Ideas

Did you ever read something, get to the bottom of the page and have absolutely no idea what you read? It happens to all of us because of the way our brains pay attention, make sense, and respond to our environment. Here are the three Big Brain Ideas:

1. There's no comprehension without picturing.
2. We make meaning by connecting to prior knowledge.
3. Neurons that fire together wire together.

Let's look further at these ideas:

1. Your brain comprehends information by picturing. If I say the word "dog" what do you see: the letters d-o-g or an image of a dog? Our brains pay attention to words in the form of pictures. If you read a page without comprehending, it's because your brain was not picturing the words.

2. Your brain makes meaning by linking new information to something familiar. Does this statement have any meaning for you: "The hurricane slammed into the Florida coast and damaged thousands of boats?" When you hear these words your brain immediately scans your memory bank to make the words meaningful: all the concepts you understand, all the vocabulary you know, and everything you've learned. If you haven't actually seen a hurricane, or the Florida coast, your brain uses symbols like wind, waves or storms to make a picture of the words.

3. Your brain works faster when you enrich it with new connections – or "Neurons that fire together wire together." Do you know your brain is a vast communication network that actually works smoother and easier the more you stimulate and use it? Neuroscientists have proven that when

you learn new things, your brain neurons fire, fire, fire to make new connections – and they form new pathways that work at a higher speed. Learning physically changes your brain because little by little you're making new and stronger connections, making it easier to go back in your brain and grab any information you need to learn something new.

Notice how the big brain ideas help you comprehend new learning skills. These skills will help you read faster, memorize anything important, learn while you're studying, be prepared for tests, get started fast on any writing assignment, make better notes, and think of lots of ideas to get what you want.

Read Fast, Comprehend More

Try this reading skill from the Upgrade Series book *Quantum Reader*.

When you first learned to read, you ran your finger along the words to keep your place. Later, you were told that this isn't the way "big people" read and that it slows you down. While it's true that most adults don't read with their fingers, it isn't because it slows them down. Studies show that using a visual guide, such as your finger or a pencil, actually speeds your reading by keeping you from backtracking.

See for yourself:

Sit face-to-face with a friend. Ask him or her to look about six inches above your head and move his eyes around your face in a circle. (He should only move his eyes – not his head.) You'll notice his eyes move in spurts and jerks – not in a smooth circle. Now, do it again, but this time, ask your friend to use his finger to trace the circle. Notice how his eyes continuously move forward with the help of a visual guide.

Move your finger just below the text you're reading, keeping your eyes just ahead of your finger. As you come to the end of a line, quickly move to the line below. Push yourself to move a little faster than is comfortable. Use your peripheral vision to take in a third of a line at once.

Today, those numinous eyes, bushy mustache, and shock of silver hair remain the quintessential image of "genius," the name a synonym for supernormal intelligence. But as a child, Albert Einstein appeared deficient. Dyslexia caused him difficulty in speech and reading.

You may stop and re-read words because you think you missed something, but if you're focused, you'll get it. You must keep moving forward to increase your reading speed. Your eyes will move faster and more efficiently when pushed along by your finger. We call this upgrade "the quick fix" because using a visual guide alone can double your reading speed.

Memorize Anything, Anytime

Try this memorizing skill from the Upgrade Series book *Quantum Memorizer*.

If it's worth remembering, it's worth taking the time to make links

Linking is a memory tool where you make a series of associations by making the visual tie that connects one item to the next, and to the next. We sometimes call linking a "narrative chain" when it is several links put together into a story. The links can be as short or as long as you want.

For example, let's say you want to remember the order of the first four presidents of the United States: George Washington, John Adams, Thomas Jefferson, and James Madison.

Create a mini story to connect the presidents' names in the right order with images of familiar (but freaky) items or situations that you can picture.

Like this: George was WASHing the ADAMS (apple) of the TOM (cat) that jumped out of his arms because it got very MAD.

It's important to be very clear about what specific items you are associating. You remember each item better by making an association to a concrete item or familiar scene in your mind that links it to the next thing you want to remember. Use this tool to memorize things that are important or of interest to you.

Make Notes Meaningful and Memorable

Try this note-taking skill from the Upgrade Series book *Quantum Note-Taker*.

Don't Just Take Notes, Make Notes

Notes:TM is a quantum note-taking technique that helps you make sense of information, recall it longer, and understand it better. In Notes: TM, the "T" stands for *taking* and the "M" stands for *making*. Notes:TM is your go-to technique for taking notes in classes or presentations of any kind.

This quantum technique keeps your whole brain busy by combining the two actions of taking notes and making notes. The note-taking part keeps you focused on the content being presented, and the note-making part keeps you interested by writing down how your own thoughts and feelings connect to what you're hearing.

By writing down what a speaker is saying and your own thoughts and feelings about what you're learning, you're focusing both your conscious and subconscious mind. Imagine yourself in this classroom situation and check out the way I record the notes to get a preview of how Notes:TM works. Then you can practice it on your own.

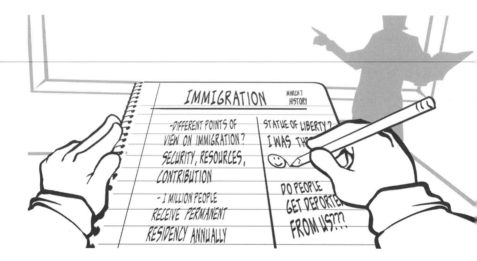

Picture this: You're listening to your teacher describe different points of view on immigration. She uses names of politicians, activists, poets, educators and immigrants. She provides historical facts, dates, laws and statistics about immigrants over the past 100 years. You're focusing on the teacher's words and writing down factual data; that's your conscious mind at work. The subconscious is where you make connections to that information. For example, you're wondering why your grandparents came to the U.S. so you make a note with their names and a question mark. You're noting information that reminds you of your own experience like your visit to the Statue of Liberty, and you're putting a little smiley face symbol by this note because it's a happy memory. You're writing questions like: What are my beliefs about immigration? Why did my grandparents change their name? And concerns like: What happens to people if they have to go back to their countries?

You can see from the notes that I can capture the facts the teacher mentions and follow my own thoughts at the same time. It's writing down your deeper thoughts that makes you aware of how you feel, what you already know, and what kind of things you like to wonder about. This keeps your brain happy because you're connecting and making meaning, the way your brain likes it. And, an added bonus: If your teacher suddenly turns to you and asks for your opinion on immigration, you're ready to respond.

C'mon, Gimme That Test!

Try these 10 test-taking strategies and you'll be saying "C'mon, gimme that test!"

1. **Know you know.** Be prepared. Practice. Simulate the exact conditions and tasks of the exam.

2. **What's it all about?** Find out the format of the test. Is it multiple choice? Essay questions? Sentence completion? Short answer? True/False? Open book?

3. **Eat it.** Your breakfast, that is. Have a healthy, light breakfast that includes some protein like eggs, lean ham or yogurt and fruit. It's great for your energy without making you sluggish.

4. **It's about comfort.** Dress in layers. You never know what the test-room temperature will be. Be ready for anything.

5. **Memorize important facts and formulas.** Write them down in margins when you first get the test.

6. **Ask your teacher.** Seriously. Ask for clarification or rephrasing of questions you don't understand. This may help trigger information in your head. *(This doesn't mean ask the teacher for the answer.)*

7. **Write it down.** Write down your reasoning, even if you don't know the exact answer. Estimate and impress your teacher with your resourcefulness. Get the partial credit.

8. **Picturing.** If you can't remember a fact, close your eyes and picture where it is in your notes, in your book, or on your Mind Map.

9. **Know your needs.** Prepare everything you need for the exam the night before.

   (For the SAT/ACT, sharpened #2 pencils, approved calculator with new batteries, sweater or sweatshirt, photo ID, admission ticket, a healthy snack, erasers, watch ...)

10. **Get psyched, stay psyched.** Talk to yourself before and during the test. Say things like: "I am ready for this test" and "I know the material and will remember it easily."

Write Easily, Less Stress, Better Results

Try this writing preparation skill from the Upgrade Series book *Quantum Writer*.

See It, Say It, Draw It

Sometimes your creative mind needs some warming up to brainstorm your ideas for writing. You can prime your creative mind at any time with this See It, Say It, Draw It exercise.

See It

To accurately describe something in words, you must first observe or "see" it carefully. In other words, good writers are also good observers. Take a few seconds to study your surroundings. When you're ready, close your eyes and picture as many details as possible: the clock on your desk, your favorite poster, an empty wastebasket – whatever you can remember. Recreate the scene in your mind. Now pick a unique item, one you may not have noticed before, like a crack in the wall or a fortune cookie. Make up a story about that item by being curious and asking questions like: How did that item get there? Who made it? When was it made? What is it for? The more ridiculous your answers, the better! For example, maybe you imagine one big fortune cookie factory where all the world's fortune cookies are made, and the message in this particular cookie was wrapped up just for you in that factory and delivered to your desk as a clue to how the rest of your life was going to turn out. *Now, take a minute to make a story for a different item in your room. It may seem silly at first, but this exercise will prime your creative mind.*

Say It

Take a closer look at the item you chose for your story. This time, describe everything you can about its actual appearance. Be as specific as possible. For example, let's say you chose a pencil on your desk. Pick it up, and talk about it. You might say: It's yellow with a few chew marks near the end. It has a tiny pinkish-tan eraser, little blue dots around the rim, weighs about two ounces, smells like dog fur, and has the word Castell on it. Hey, maybe there's a big pencil-making factory, too! *Now describe the item you selected.*

Draw It

Drawing the item from your story will further boost your observation skills by helping your mind remember more details. Like the See It and Say It parts of the exercise, drawing a picture is all about narrowing the gap between your thoughts and your writing by getting your mind ready to move, maneuver and make the jump to the page. Your picture stimulates new words and ideas you can use for your writing. *Make a drawing of the item you selected and described.*

Think Bigger, Make Things Happen

Try this thinking skill from the Upgrade Series book *Quantum Thinker*.

Get Lots and Lots of Ideas

Like shopping at a superstore or buying a bunch of raffle tickets, improving the selection and number of ideas in your head increases the chances you'll come across the right one.

According to inventor Dr. Yoshio Nakamata, holder of twenty-three hundred patents, people who want to think bigger should stuff their brain. "Keep pumping information into it," he says. "Give your brain lots of raw material. Then give it a chance to cook."

Get more ideas in your head by resisting the urge to judge every thought and idea that comes your way. Remember, you have permission to think whatever you want. But you don't have to say everything that pops into your head. In fact, it's probably a good idea not to! Another important thing to remember when stuffing your brain is that you can try ideas on for size.

You don't need to believe 100% in an idea just to think it.

Quantum learners have skills for academic excellence.

Use these core skills to build lots of success moments so you feel more confident about learning new things and going after what you want in your life.

Know It When You Need It

Have you ever been in a situation like taking a test or answering a question in class where you know that you know something but you just can't get the information from your brain when you need it? This is because the information did not stick in your mind. If this happens to you, or you just want to get at the knowledge you already have more easily, use the Success Model for studying. It reinforces and helps cement information in your brain.

The **Success Model** combines three actions: Chunk information, make it multisensory (picture it, talk it, act it) and review it. These three actions help move information into your long-term memory so you can know it when you need it.

One of the things that signals your brain to store information where you can "reach" it is review. When your brain is bombarded with the same information again and again, it starts to get the message that this information is probably important enough to store permanently. A great way to review is **Circuit Learning**, a study review scheduling system.

Here's how Circuit Learning works:

First you need to define the total content you plan to learn. Let's say you need to learn 120 vocabulary words. Next you chunk the information into "workable" pieces. If you have ten days to learn the 120 vocabulary words, you could chunk them into eight groups of 15 words each, leaving the last two days to review all the chunks. The next step is to assign a letter to each chunk of 15 words, so chunk A would be words 1 to 15, chunk B would be words 16 to 30, etc. up to chunk H for words 106 to 120. Now you can set up your written study review schedule.

> Circuit: a circular journey beginning and ending at the same place

On Monday spend 30 minutes learning chunk A. On Tuesday you would spend 10 minutes reviewing chunk A followed by 20 minutes learning chunk B. On Wednesday, spend 5 minutes reviewing chunk A, 10 minutes reviewing chunk B, and 15 minutes learning chunk C. On Thursday, it would be 5 minutes on B, 10 minutes on C, and 15 minutes on D. This process continues until day 9 when you spend 5 minutes reviewing chunk H followed by 25 minutes reviewing chunks A to E, and day 10 when you spend 40 minutes reviewing chunks A to H. The next day you ace your test! Here's what your study review schedule will look like:

Monday	Tuesday	Wednesday	Thursday	Friday
Date:				
30 min. A	10 min. A	5 min. A	5 min. B	5 min. C
		10 min. B	10 min. C	10 min. D
	20 min. B	15 min C	15 min D	15 min. E

For more complicated subjects, chunk the content into meaningful sections and assign letters to the chunks according to priority, A being the highest priority chunk. For example, if you were preparing for a history test you could chunk the content into sections by years, or even by chapters. If you were preparing for a test on a country, you could chunk the content by subject, such as geography, natural resources, culture, etc., and split subjects that are too big into two or more chunks.

Date:

	Monday	Tuesday	Wednesday	Thursday	Friday
	30 min. A	10 min. A	5 min. A	5 min. B	5 min. C
		20 min. B	10 min. B	10 min. C	10 min. D
			15 min. C	15 min. D	15 min. E

Date:

	Monday	Tuesday	Wednesday	Thursday	Friday
	5 min. D	5 min. E	5 min. F	5 min. H	40 min. A
	10 min. E	10 min. F	10 min. G	25 min. A	B
	15 min. F	15 min. G	15 min. H	B	C
				C	D
				D	E
				E	F
					G
					H

Priority*   **Content to Learn**

*Priority: List important content to study. Make your list A–H, A being highest priority.

Permission to copy chart from Quantum Learning Network

64

You can use Circuit Learning for up to twelve chunks (more would be difficult to review on one circuit), for any timeframe (you can even put a weekly chart on the wall), and for any subject. Just remember to chunk it (make it bite size), make it multisensory (so your brain can see, hear and feel it), and review it (so your brain knows it by heart), to move it into long-term memory.

Study Space Makeover

You spend a lot of time studying, so why not take ownership for your study space?

Upgrading your learning skills also means paying attention to your entire studying and learning experience the same way you'd prepare for a road trip. Do you have the right environment, music space? Do you have enough room and the right seating for comfort and concentration? Do you know where you're going and what you want to accomplish? Whether it's acing a test, or writing an impressive paper for your history class, you'll get better mileage and enjoy the ride if you're ready to keep cruising.

A few other things to consider
for your study area

- A bulletin board where you can put visual aids like charts, lists or pictures
- A shelf for books and reference materials
- A notebook or tape recorder to capture thoughts and ideas
- A daily planner to organize your time
- Awards and certificates that remind you of previous success moments
- A stereo or other music system

Here's how to do it:

First, claim some space. Unlike the special place you picture yourself in when you get into alpha state, this is a real place. Choose a quiet place like your bedroom, or a spare room, den or attic – anywhere that you can head off distractions and have control of the space. (Harry Potter's space under the stairs is a little cramped but it's his very own.) Next, try to pull

together a combination of furniture that fits your style. Think of a time when you were able to concentrate easily and do a great amount of work without stress and recreate it. Lighting is also important. The space should be well lit without hurting your eyes. Check out a few different lighting schemes around your house, at school, or at the library so you know what you want.

Relaxation induced by specific music leaves the mind alert and able to concentrate. Baroque music works best. It may not be the same playlist you'll use for your next road trip to the beach, but a little Bach, Handel or Vivaldi will definitely get you in the learning groove.

Some things you just can't explain. For example, you may have heard that if you play Pink Floyd's *Dark Side of the Moon* album backwards while watching *The Wizard of Oz* – starting both at the same time – the two synch up perfectly. Strange but true! Baroque music has a similar unexplainable element to its composition. Baroque composers used specific beat patterns that automatically synchronize our minds and our bodies. For instance, most baroque music is timed at around sixty beats per minute, which is the same as an average resting heart rate – the same heart rate you need for alpha state. Many contemporary musicians are amazed at how their peers could have possibly achieved such precision.

Now that you're ready to hit the road, think of where you want to go. You wouldn't take a road trip around the block or to someplace you go every day. After all, the whole point of a road trip is to try something new, to get out of your comfort zone – the same is true with learning. You have to take a risk to get what you want.

Chapter 4:

Take Charge of Your Life

[████████████████████░░░░░░░]

Your upgrade is 75% complete

Do you build yourself up or tear yourself down? Do you let things happen to you or do you take charge of what happens and let your voice be heard? Taking charge of your life begins to happen when you realize you can control how you feel, think and act. No one else is responsible. Only you!

Do you remember the first big thing you saved up for and bought with your own money? Whether it was a bike, iPod, book or a gift for someone, you didn't just bring it home and throw it in the closet. You took care of it and took responsibility for it.

For example, let's say you bought a bike. As a take-charge owner, you would also get a helmet so you could use it with a sense of adventure and fearlessness. This way you could go faster, explore more of the neighborhood, and enjoy greater independence.

Taking charge of something means that you're accountable for what happens to it. This is true whether it's a bike, or your life. When you take charge of your life, you own everything that happens to you. You give your best effort to get the results you want.

Get an Excellent Life
Realize that you drive your life.
Be your own best friend.
Build yourself up.

There are all sorts of ways to take charge of your life. Eight of them stand out as universal keys to living an excellent life, with more chances to be proud of yourself and get your best results.

The 8 Keys of Excellence

- **Integrity** – your behavior lines up with your values so you feel authentic and sincere
- **Failure Leads to Success** – you learn from things that don't go well the first time
- **Speak with Good Purpose** – you talk with positive intent in a direct and honest way
- **This Is It!** – you focus your attention on the moment to get the most out of it
- **Commitment** – you follow through on goals and dreams you make important in your life
- **Ownership** – you take responsibility for your actions
- **Flexibility** – you shift your thinking and make changes to get better results
- **Balance** – you spend time on the most important things in your life

Quantum learners take responsibility for their lives.

Living and learning are not orderly step-by-step processes and neither are the keys to living an excellent life. That's why they're so powerful – they fit your life. They help run your life in a way that is true to who you are and what you want. *Here's how they work:*

Live your life every moment with **Integrity**. Living with integrity means that your behaviors line up with your values. Values can be as simple as being honest with your friends. When your behavior reflects this value, you're living with integrity. For example, let's say you tell a friend that they should try out for a play, but you mention to someone else that you don't think they will get the part. That's not living with integrity. Your values and behavior are not in synch.

Because life is full of learning opportunities, there will be times when you fail. How you respond to this failure is the key to refocusing your energy. When you fail, it's important to know that **Failure Leads to Success**. Let's say you failed to be selected as a writer for your school newsletter because you turned in old stories and were afraid to write anything new. You can turn this experience into a future success by realizing that you need to give your best effort even when you're in the learning zone to get something you really want. In other words, use your failure as feedback. Think about what you'll do differently to get better results.

Let's say you're losing interest in learning because one of your teachers only calls on the boys in the class and seems to ignore you. You can be effective telling someone about something that's bothering you if you **Speak with Good Purpose**. Let your teacher know that there is something he can do to help you do even better in class. Tell him that you come to class every day ready to participate but class time is short and he seems to call on other people and not get around to you. Be honest and direct about what you want.

Life is made up of little moments when we choose to pay attention to what we can take charge of, or not. **This Is It!** is your take-charge attitude for focusing all your attention on the present moment. So if you're feeling like you're having a bad day and things are out of your control, reach for your This Is It! attitude and make more moments turn out the way you want them to.

Have you ever committed to something and then lost interest and not followed through? Have you let others down? Have you let yourself down? Think of each **Commitment** you make as a promise to yourself or to someone else, and don't make it unless you're 100% into doing it. Commitment is about doing *whatever it takes* (WIT) to keep your word and achieve your goals.

If you tell a friend you'll meet him at a certain time but you're two hours late because you were hanging out with another friend, don't make excuses. Take ownership by saying, "I was wrong not to meet you as planned or call you." **Ownership** is about being someone who can be counted on and taking responsibility for the choices you make.

Flexibility is a key to your sanity. It's about not getting locked in to only one way. If you're trying to achieve something (like getting up on time in the morning) and it's just not working, try another way (move the alarm clock to the other side of the room so you have to get up to shut it off). Changing what you're doing can give you a better outcome, but you'll never know until you try.

Some people say that you shouldn't make a big decision when you're standing on one leg. They mean you need both feet planted firmly so you are thinking and acting from a place of **Balance**. Think about your daily schedule of school, other lessons, family, friends and interests. Now think about how you prioritize what matters most to you. Then focus on doing what's important in your life every day to get the results you want. This will keep your feet planted and your energy in balance.

You can take these 8 Keys with you wherever you go. When you do, you'll take responsibility for everything that happens to you.

Checking in with yourself by using these 8 Keys is a lifelong way to be your own best friend, build yourself up, and take charge of what happens next in your life.

Quantum learners know how to set and achieve goals.

Here's an example of how you might use all 8 Keys.

Let's say you're preparing for an upcoming test. Focus your energy and take control of the outcome with the 8 Keys. Think about the last test you took in this subject. If it didn't go as well as you would have liked, think about what you'll do differently this time. Remember that *failure leads to success*. If you start to dwell on how difficult the last exam was, remind yourself that *this is it!* Even though it may be difficult, now is the time to go for it. Stay *flexible* and make a new study plan using your chunk and review skills. Make a *commitment* to a better grade by setting up a study group of responsible classmates who will support each another. Use your awareness of learning styles to study better alone and learn from other group members, and *speak with good purpose* when communicating your ideas, even if others may not agree with them. Take *ownership* for your productivity by being someone who can be counted on. Use your *integrity* to resist any urges to cut corners along the way. And remember to stay *balanced* by focusing on what's important – and celebrate your success!

Every situation will be different, but these 8 Keys will help you run your life like a best friend guiding you along, keeping you on track – and that best friend is YOU!

Your upgrade is 100% complete

Your brain is a storehouse of
natural learning energy
and experiences. Learning is
everything you do with it.

Congratulations!
You're a Quantum Learner

As a quantum learner, you know how to get into learning, get the facts, get more skills, and get an excellent life. You give your best effort to get your best results because you've got learning skills to accomplish anything. You know how you're smart and how you learn best so you can rearrange your energy, your attitude, your plan, and your actions to get what you want.

You can read, write, memorize, take tests, study, make notes, think bigger, and learn better than when you started this book. This means that starting now you can turn every opportunity to learn and perform into a successful experience just by the way you think about it, get ready for it, and take charge. You are the sculptor of your life experiences and you know how to focus your learning energy to get more of the things you want.

About the Author

Bobbi DePorter
Bobbi DePorter is the cofounder of SuperCamp and president of Quantum Learning Network (QLN). Based in Oceanside, California, QLN is a global education leader impacting more than 2 million youth and adults from 50 states and 80 countries with programs for personal and academic excellence. Her previous books include *Quantum Success*, *Quantum Teaching*, *Quantum Learning* and *The Seven Biggest Teen Problems And How To Turn Them Into Strengths*, and have been printed in seven languages with worldwide distribution.

Books by Bobbi DePorter

The Quantum Upgrade Series
Quantum Learner
Quantum Reader
Quantum Writer
Quantum Memorizer
Quantum Thinker
Quantum Note-Taker

Quantum Success: 8 Key Catalysts to Shift Your Energy into Dynamic Focus
Quantum Business: Achieving Success through Quantum Learning
Quantum Teaching: Orchestrating Student Success
Quantum Learning: Unleashing the Genius in You
The 8 Keys of Excellence: Principles to Live By
The Seven Biggest Teen Problems And How To Turn Them Into Strengths

How to Contact the Quantum Learning Network

By Phone: (760) 722-0072
By Mail: Quantum Learning Network
     1938 Avenida del Oro
     Oceanside, CA 92056

Online: www.QLN.com

Receive your complimentary *"I am a Quantum Learner"* poster at www.QuantumLearner.com.

International associate offices in Taiwan, China, Hong Kong, South Korea, Malaysia, Singapore, Indonesia, Mexico, Dominican Republic and Switzerland